tmi

me, my friends, and

more than I really **need** to know!

by T. Bugbird

Designed by Annie Simpson

with thanks to the students of Bridgewater School
and Mia Hazell Liyanage

too much
information!

tmi

Ever opened your mouth and spilled out just

too much information?

Then get ready to share the **shame!**

Take a solo survey or **fess up** with your **friends**. Will you keep your **cool** or be **beaten** by a **blush?**

Texting is better than talking.

You love to chat with your friends and are not always the most discreet person, but you know when to pull a break on the gossip.

I love to spread scandal.

Gossip can be fun, but maybe you don't realize that sometimes it can be wrong and very hurtful. Next time you are going to blab, think: would you like it if someone said that about you?

It's ok to talk about someone behind their back.

You don't like to gossip and know when to keep it zipped. This makes you a super-trustworthy friend!

false

true

false

true

true

false

shrug or shriek!

How much embarrassment can you take?
Follow the flow – will you shriek or shrug?
If you shrug 'cuz you just don't care, go on to the
next space. If you shriek with embarrassment,
follow the pink arrow for your assessment!

It's your best friend's party...

start here

You've arrived half an hour late.

Your dad drives you and insists on coming in to say "hi" to your friend's mom.

It's understandable that you're worried about this situation. You've done well to stay so relaxed up to this point, but it's a shame you couldn't hold it together a little longer.

It doesn't take much for you to bag a blush! This could be the cause of a cringe, but try to relax – things could be much worse, believe me!

You're wearing the same outfit as your friend's little sister!

Your dad is still at the party, and now he's doing the superman dance to the Jonas Brothers – with your friend's mom!

Eew! Your shriek is not only understandable but a natural response to a truly cringe-creating situation. It's time to go, but you've shown you can take more embarrassment than most!

Ooh, this is getting difficult. Maybe it is time to quit (or at least hide in the bathroom for ten minutes). You've kept your cool up til now – good job!

Your crush has just noticed you're wearing the same outfit as your BFF's sister (except she hasn't spilled chocolate all over herself), and he's telling everyone!

You try to laugh, but it comes out wrong and you spray chocolate shake out of your nose. Double gross!

Uh-oh, your crush saw that!

You spill a chocolate shake on your outfit, and it looks gross!

This situation is truly a disaster. If you are still shruggin', then kudos to you and your inner calm. If not, maybe your dad's still around for a ride home . . .

Your secret crush is at the party, and he's talking to your dad!

wheel of shame!

Got a secret blush? Then it's time to fess up IN FRONT of your friends! First, answer one of the questions in the small circles; this will give you a number. Work your way clockwise around the wheel, starting at the yellow segment, until you land on your question. Do you dare to share, or is it totally TMI?

Take your age and add three.

Add up the digits of your house or apartment number. (So, if it's 74 then 7 + 4 = 11.)

What number day of the week is it? (If it's Sunday, the number is one.)

On what day of the month were you born?

How many pets do you have? (If the answer is none, take the yellow segment.)

Take your age and subtract six.

How many letters are there in your first name?

How many people are in your house right now?

How many times can you snap your fingers in five seconds? (Get a friend to time you!)

How many people are there in your family?

wheel of **shame!**

Do you ever sing in the shower?

Confess your secret nickname.

Have you ever passed gas in class?

Describe your craziest hairstyle ever.

What's the most revolting thing you have ever eaten?

Name your most embarrassing celebrity crush.

Who's your secret school crush?

Describe your worst underwear!

would you rather...

have $20 to spend today	or	**$100 to spend next year?**
walk into class wearing a clown's nose	or	walk into class in a tutu?
eat a worm sandwich	or	**eat a snail sandwich?**
wear nothing but orange	or	wear nothing but purple?
wash a dog	or	**wash a car?**
have your hair cut by your dad	or	have your hair cut by your best friend?
drink nothing but milk for a week	or	**drink nothing but pineapple juice for a week?**
sing with your mom in class	or	dance with your dad at your party?

If you **really, really**

wear old-fashioned shoes	or	wear an old-fashioned hat?
lose your watch	or	**lose your diary?**
sleep on a bed of crackers	or	sleep on a bed of potato chips?
be a rabbit for a day	or	**be a cat for a day?**
star in *Joseph*	or	star in *Grease*?
ride to school on a tractor	or	**ride to school on an elephant?**
tie pasta shells in your hair	or	tie candy canes in your hair?
have three brothers	or	**have three sisters?**

had to **choose!!!**

fact or fancy ?

Take turns answering the questions. The twist is that you DON'T have to tell the truth! Give your answers (the more details the better), and then have your friends guess whether you're dishing up Fact or Fancy!

Have you ever pretended to feel ill to avoid eating vegetables?

What's the most embarrassing TV show you still secretly like to watch?

What's the scariest thing that's ever bitten you?

Who would be your celebrity BFF?

Describe the funniest hat you've ever worn.

If you could be any animal, what would you be?

What did you dream about last night?

Have you ever tried fake tanning lotion and turned totally orange?

What's the weirdest thing you have ever styled your hair with?

Have you ever cut your own hair? **Rocking or shocking?**

If you could swap places with any celebrity, who would it be?

Who's your strangest relative?

Do you prefer the town or the country? Why?

Would you ever get a tattoo? Where?

If you could be any book character, who would you be?

What's the worst ringtone you've ever heard?

Have you ever kept your coat on because you hated what you were wearing underneath?

Have you ever kissed a picture of your celebrity crush?

Have you ever tried on your mom's clothes when she wasn't around?

Have you ever sneezed on a stranger?

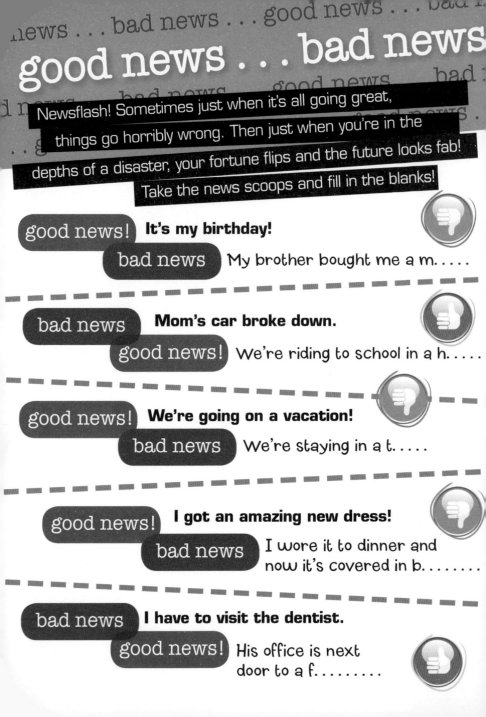

good news . . . bad news

Newsflash! Sometimes just when it's all going great, things go horribly wrong. Then just when you're in the depths of a disaster, your fortune flips and the future looks fab! Take the news scoops and fill in the blanks!

good news! **It's my birthday!**

bad news My brother bought me a m.....

---

bad news **Mom's car broke down.**

good news! We're riding to school in a h.....

---

good news! **We're going on a vacation!**

bad news We're staying in a t.....

---

good news! **I got an amazing new dress!**

bad news I wore it to dinner and now it's covered in b........

---

bad news **I have to visit the dentist.**

good news! His office is next door to a f........

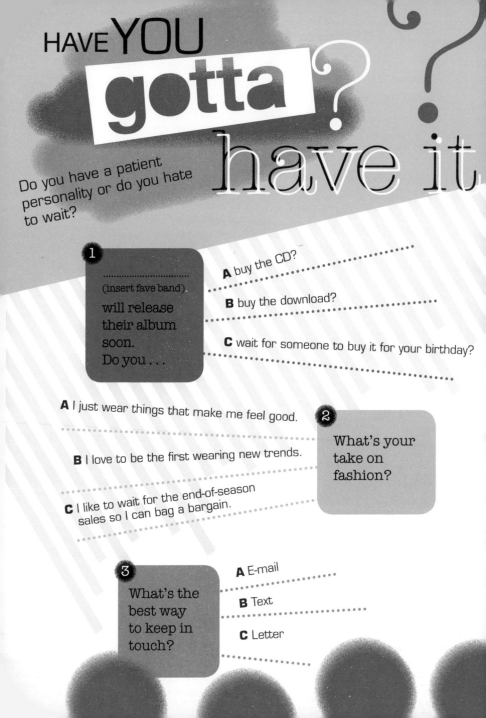

HAVE **YOU** *gotta* ? have it

Do you have a patient personality or do you hate to wait?

1

.... (insert fave band)
will release their album soon.
Do you . . .

A buy the CD?

B buy the download?

C wait for someone to buy it for your birthday?

A I just wear things that make me feel good.

B I love to be the first wearing new trends.

C I like to wait for the end-of-season sales so I can bag a bargain.

2

What's your take on fashion?

3

What's the best way to keep in touch?

A E-mail

B Text

C Letter

A Hot chocolate

4

Need to fix a drink? What's your pick?

B Water or a fizzy drink

C Homemade smoothie

5

Holiday of a lifetime – is it . . .

A flying to a faraway country?

B an extreme sports camp?

C going on a cruise?

A A cat

6

Which animal are you most like?

B A puppy

C A tortoise

Mostly A's

You've got a great, balanced attitude. You're no slouch when it comes to action, but you know that sometimes the most rewarding results aren't instant.

Mostly B's

You hate to waste time, and that's a good thing. But slow down a minute! Your grab-and-go attitude is great for instant results, but are they always the best?

Mostly C's

If you were a shoe, you'd be a casual loafer. You like to take things easy, and if that means that sometimes you miss the bus, who cares? It's cool not to stress, but don't forget there's a time for action too!

good day  bad day

The following situations could have any outcome. Think of the best that could happen (good day) and the worst (bad day).

Happy ending or totally TMI!!

---

good day

It's the first day of the school year, and you're taking a seat in class. Your crush comes and sits next to you. What happens next?

bad day

---

good day

You ask your hairstylist to make you look like a pop star! You come out of the salon looking like . . .

bad day

---

good day

The mailman has delivered a big package just for you! What's inside?

bad day

You're having a sleepover with your best friends. Someone knocks on your bedroom door just as you are having a snack. Who is it?

good day

bad day

Your parents organize a "special" birthday treat for you. What is it?

good day

bad day

You're taking a cooking class and are told you will be preparing a meal for a special guest. Who is it?

good day

bad day

Your aunt has given you tickets for a concert next Saturday. Who will you be rocking out to?

good day

bad day

Your dad's taking you to school in his new car. What is it?

good day

bad day

You put your hand down the side of your couch to see if there's anything there. What do you find?

good day

bad day

Your mom has dyed her hair! What's the color?

good day

bad day

would you rather..?

ride a camel	or	**ride a giraffe?**
eat cornflakes without milk	or	eat toast without butter?
walk barefoot in the snow	or	**walk barefoot in the mud?**
learn to surf	or	learn to ski?
wear a ball gown on the beach	or	**wear a swimsuit in the supermarket?**
wear boots in the summer	or	wear flip-flops in the winter?
have a pet slug	or	**have a pet jellyfish?**
be famous	or	be rich?

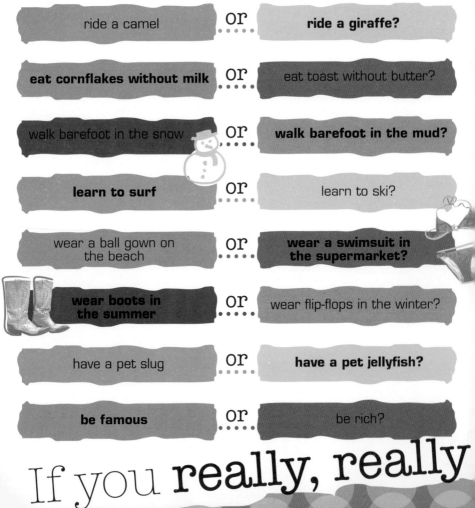

If you **really, really**

sing in front of your class or have your mom sing in front of your class?

have one big present or **have lots of small presents?**

hold a tarantula or hold a worm?

have no TV for a year or **have no cell phone for a year?**

clean your brother's bedroom or have extra math homework for a week?

wear too-big shoes or **wear too-big shorts?**

walk backwards for a day or not speak for a day?

drink frog soup or **eat bat jello?**

had to **choose!!!**

all star tmi

Sometimes the rich and fabulous just tell you **TOO MUCH!**

1) Flip through your favorite magazine.

2) Find a pic of your favorite (or least favorite!) celeb. Cut it out and paste it in the box.

3) Fill the speech bubbles with what YOU think they're saying!

mall

school

or friend's house ?

Check out the situation, and then decide the **best** place and the **worst** place it could happen from the three choices.

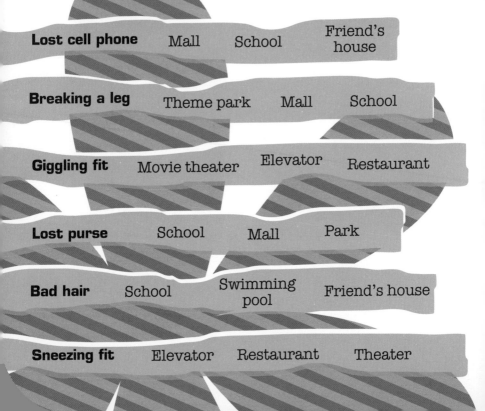

| **Lost cell phone** | Mall | School | Friend's house |

| **Breaking a leg** | Theme park | Mall | School |

| **Giggling fit** | Movie theater | Elevator | Restaurant |

| **Lost purse** | School | Mall | Park |

| **Bad hair** | School | Swimming pool | Friend's house |

| **Sneezing fit** | Elevator | Restaurant | Theater |

Passing gas   Restaurant   On the bus   Friend's house

Argument with your best friend   On the bus   School   Theme park

Argument with your mom   School   Mall   Friend's house

No toilet paper   School   Restaurant   Swimming pool

Having smelly feet   Theater   Elevator   On the bus

Runny nose and no handkerchief   Restaurant   Movie theater   Dentist's

Unexpectedly meet your crush   Mall   Friend's house   On the bus

Have a big blemish on your nose   Restaurant   School   Hair salon

Wearing bad shoes   School   Park   Theme park

A hiccup fit   Restaurant   Dentist's   Movie theater

Walking in on someone using the restroom   School   Restaurant   Friend's house

ARE **YOU** STUNNED BY

surprises ?

Will you be derailed by unexpected turns?

1 You forgot your gym bag, and your teacher makes you take the class in your underwear! What's your first thought?

A Phew! At least I'm wearing my best set!

B Maybe if I wish hard enough the gym will burn down before class starts.

C Duh! I'd better remember it next time!

2 You are talking with your friend's mom, and out of nowhere you let out a loud burp! What's the first thing you say?

A Pardon me!

B Eeeew! I think your cat's got gas!

C Bet you can't do that!

3 You're having a sleepover with your friends, and your mom has just crashed your party with an album full of your baby photos. What do you say?

A Okay, okay, but make it quick.

B Open that album and I'll never come out of my room again, ever!

C I so rocked Baby Gap!

A ask if you can borrow a spare pair of jeans and a tee-shirt?

B turn around, run, and call your dad to come and pick you up NOW?

decide the Snickers look kind of rocks in a Lady Gaga sort of way?

4

You've arrived at your friend's party dressed as a Snickers bar. She decided against fancy dress and forgot to tell you! Do you . . .

Mostly A's

You understand that you can never quite predict what will happen next and keep your calm in most situations. Your super-serene outlook makes you a fantastic friend when your buddies are bothered by blushes!

5

You knock on your friend's door expecting her to answer, but it's her totally cute brother instead. What do you do?

A Ask if his sister's in and think of something interesting to talk about while you're waiting.

B Feel really awkward and start giggling for no reason whatsoever.

C Ask him out on a date.

Mostly B's

You sometimes find it hard to cope when life takes a terrible twist, but when you're caught by a cringe, think: "Is it really so bad?" Focus on something positive, and you'll be amazed how quickly the moment passes!

A How thoughtful of everyone to come!

B Cringe! Let the ground swallow me up now!

C Cool – I love parties!

6

It's your birthday. You arrive home from school and "Surprise!" your parents have secretly arranged a party for you. What's your first thought?

Mostly C's

Nothing really surprises you and you always seem to have a cute comment to counter any potential cringe. But are you really that confident, or is all that sass hiding a more serious side?

OMG
oh my gosh!

Bag a blush or brush it off? Read these stories, and you be the judge!

MORTIFYING MAGAZINE!

" I was at the local store and decided to buy my favorite magazine. As a treat, I also picked up a mag for my baby sis. As I was leaving the store, I tripped on the step. The magazines fell out of my bag just as my crush was entering the store. He looked down and saw the *Fairy Magic Magazine* for my sis and assumed it was mine! I was so embarrassed! "

Totally shameful?   **Fair cause for a blush?**   **Oh, puh-lease! Get over it!**

BOWLING BLUSH

" Last week, my friends and I went to the bowling alley as a treat for my birthday. When we arrived, they had run out of shoes my size, so I had to wear some that were a bit too big. Since it was my birthday, I was the first to play. I lined myself up, and as I bowled, I flipped my left foot back. Unfortunately, my shoe was so loose that it flew off my foot and landed in the next alley where my brother was playing with his totally cute friends! They had to stop their game as I crossed over into their alley to get my shoe back! It was so embarrassing! "

Totally shameful?   **Fair cause for a blush?**   **Oh, puh-lease! Get over it!**

CROCHET SHAME!

"Usually I love it when my fave aunt comes to our house, but on my last birthday she arrived with a crocheted jacket that was big enough for two people! It was orange and had big pink letters on the back spelling out my name! Of course, I told her the nasty knit was lovely, so she insisted that I wear it out to dinner at our local restaurant. As though that wasn't mortifying enough, when I went to the restroom, the door handle got caught in one of the holes in my jacket. I pulled hard to break free, the handle came off, and I fell backwards into the salad bar! When I got up I was covered in Thousand Island dressing, and all the waiters were laughing!"

Totally shameful?   Fair cause for a blush?   Oh, puh-lease! Get over it!

SPORTS DAY DISASTER!

"I was really excited to be taking part in my town's mini-marathon. My mom made sure my best shorts and track top were super clean. In order to look my best, I decided to change into my sports gear when I arrived at the event. OMG! I had ten minutes until the start of the race, and I realized my mom had packed my little sister's shorts! I had to wear them anyway, despite the fact they were way too small. Ten minutes into the run, the shorts ripped and everyone could see my underwear!"

Oh, puh-lease! Get over it!

Totally shameful?   Fair cause for a blush?

good day

bad day

Happy ending or totally TMI!!

You've been given tickets to watch a TV show being taped. What's the show?

good day

bad day

A real-life celebrity is going to visit your school! Who is it?

good day

bad day

It's pouring rain so you open your umbrella. What happens next?

good day

bad day

Your parents decided to raise your allowance on one condition. What is it?

good day

bad day

You're going to a fancy-dress party.
What's the theme?

good day
bad day

Your dad bought a new shirt.
Describe the style.

good day
bad day

You're going on a family outing. Where to?

good day
bad day

At a restaurant, you order the "soup of the day."
What kind is it?

good day
bad day

Your grandma has a surprise for you!
What is it?

good day
bad day

It's your birthday, and you have one present
left to open. What's in the box?

good day
bad day

would you
? rather...

be a TV star for a day ...or... **be a rock star for a day?**

drink a banana and broccoli smoothie or drink a chocolate and cheese smoothie?

watch *Camp Rock* nonstop for 12 hours ...or... **watch *High School Musical* nonstop for 12 hours?**

have a film made of your life or have a book written about your life?

be invisible for a day ...or... **be famous for a day?**

wear your jeans too short or wear your jeans too long?

hold a spider or **hold a fish?**

live in a cave or live on a boat?

If you really, really

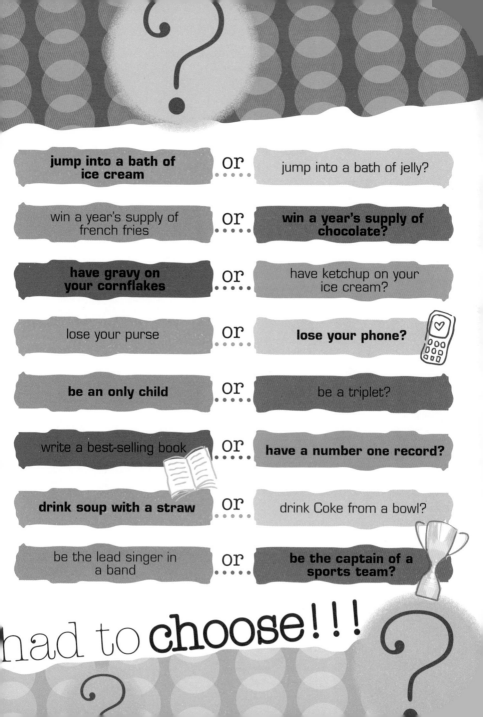

jump into a bath of ice cream	or	jump into a bath of jelly?
win a year's supply of french fries	or	**win a year's supply of chocolate?**
have gravy on your cornflakes	or	have ketchup on your ice cream?
lose your purse	or	**lose your phone?**
be an only child	or	be a triplet?
write a best-selling book	or	**have a number one record?**
drink soup with a straw	or	drink Coke from a bowl?
be the lead singer in a band	or	**be the captain of a sports team?**

had to **choose**!!!

cringe man

Just like regular hangman, you need two players.
Take one of the sentences below and think of a word to fill the gap. Next, put a dash for each letter under one of the "cringe men." Your opponent has to guess the word by gradually revealing the letters. Each time they guess a letter correctly fill in a dash, and when they get it wrong draw over one of the faint cringeman lines. If they guess the word before the cringeman is complete, they win – if they don't, you win!

Uh-oh! Mom's coming into school, and she's wearing an orange _____!

Just when I thought it couldn't get worse, I found a rip in my best _____!

I was sooo embarrassed when my dad came home riding a _____.

Eeeew! There's a _____ in my salad!

Oh no! I've been walking around school all day with _____ stuck to my shoe!

Revolting! The trash can smelled like rotting _____!

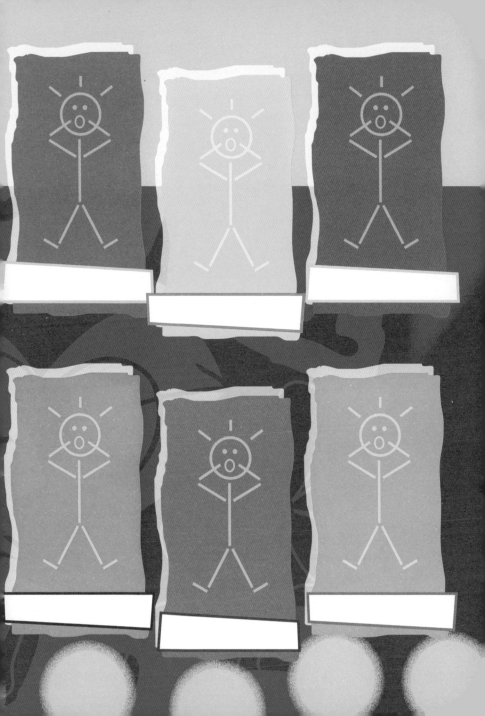

wheel of shame!

Got a secret blush? Then it's time to fess up IN FRONT of your friends! First, answer one of the questions in the small circles; this will give you a number. Work your way clockwise around the wheel, starting at the pink segment, until you land on your question. Do you dare to share, or is it totally TMI?

Take your age and add two.

How many members are there in your favorite band?

How many pairs of shoes do you have?

What number month of the year is it? (If it's June, the answer is six.)

Take the number of pets you have and add five!

Take your age and subtract two.

How many letters are there in your last name?

How many chairs can you see right now?

How many jumping jacks can you do in ten seconds? Get someone to time you!

What school year are you in?

wheel of **shame!**

Describe your craziest ever fancy dress outfit.

Did you ever wear a hat all day to hide a horrid haircut?

Did you ever run out of underwear and have to wear your brother's instead?

What's the longest time you've ever spent on the phone?

Confess your most embarrassing crush blush.

Demonstrate the most embarrassing dance you've ever seen!

Describe when you blushed the brightest red.

Which member of your family has the craziest hair?

fact or fancy?

Take turns answering the questions. The twist is that you **DON'T** have to tell the truth! Give your answers (the more details the better), and then have your friends guess whether you're dishing up **Fact or Fancy!**

Do you have a photo of your crush?

Describe the weirdest dream you have ever had.

Ever pretended you were older or younger?

What's the dumbest trick anyone has played on you?

What are your parents' middle names?

Have you ever been to the recording of a TV show?

Ever broken something and then hidden it, hoping no one would notice?

Ever had a pet bug?

Have you ever pretended to have an injury?

Have you ever changed seats to be nearer to a cute boy?

Ever tried to pluck your eyebrows?

Have you ever accidentally sent a text to the wrong person?

If you could only wear one color, what would it be?

Do you have a hidden scar?

Ever dressed up in your sister's clothes?

Ever phoned your crush and hung up before saying anything?

Is your mom's hair its natural color?

What name would you choose if you were a boy?

Ever got to the checkout line in a store and realized that you didn't have enough money?

Have you ever returned a gift for a refund?

What's the most random thing under your bed?

Do you always give 100% to whatever you are doing?

yes

no

no

Do you get homesick?

yes

Can you take criticism?

yes

no

Do you believe dreams can come true?

no

no

Well if you've got the talent, you've certainly got what it takes to shine! Say hello to Hollywood!

Maybe you're not 100% realistic, but you have a positive attitude and believe a dream is worth hanging on to! Work hard and go for it!

You might like the idea of being famous, but life in the spotlight really isn't for you. And that's totally cool! Find the thing you love to do and just do it!

OMG

Oh my gosh!

Bag a blush or brush it off? Read these stories, and you be the judge!

TERRIBLE TEXTING!

"I was texting my friend to arrange our sleepover. We decided to paint each other's nails, so I sent a message to ask her favorite color. Unfortunately, I was scrolling down my address book too fast and hit my crush's number by mistake! Ten minutes later I got a text back saying his favorite color was green!"

Totally shameful?   Fair cause for a blush?   Oh, puh-lease! Get over it!

MOM MIX-UP!

"It was my mom's birthday, so we decided to have a girl's day out shopping in town. When we got to my favorite store, we decided to split up, so I thought it would be a good time to buy my mom a surprise present. While she was in another part of the store, I bought her a cute little necklace and asked the clerk to put it in a gift box for me. I looked around for my mom and, seeing her bright red coat, I decided to creep up and surprise her. Before she had time to turn around, I locked her in a bear hug and planted a big kiss on her cheek. Then she turned around and – OMG – it wasn't my mom! It was some totally random person I'd never met before, who happened to be wearing the same coat! She looked at me as though I was a nut, while my mom and the clerk couldn't stop laughing! 100% cringe!"

Totally shameful?   Fair cause for a blush?   Oh, puh-lease! Get over it!

HORRIBLE HAIR DAY!

"I read on the Internet that if you mix water and sugar, you can make your own hair gel. Since I was bored with my do and wanted a new look, I decided to give it a try. The sugar mix was a bit sticky, but I managed to get my hair in a fierce, retro, punky style, and when it dried out it got really stiff. Somehow I sneaked onto the bus without my mom seeing what I'd done. All my friends were really impressed, but unfortunately they kept touching my hair. As my best friend was touching my sugary spikes, the bus went over a bump and she accidentally crushed them, creating a sugar shower all over my face! To try to get my style back, I tipped some water over my head, but it just turned the sugar into sticky syrup. It looked really terrible! When I got to school my teacher made me take a shower to wash the gunk out of my hair! I was sooo embarrassed!"

Totally shameful?   Fair cause for a blush?   Oh, puh-lease! Get over it!

PUPPY LOVE!

"We have a really cute puppy called Sweet Pea. One day I was taking her for a walk in the park with my big brother. We decided to have a game of fetch, so I took her off her leash. Just as I let her go, she saw some other puppies and ran over to see them. I was shouting, "Over here, Sweet Pea," just as my brother's best friend was coming towards us on his bike. He gave me a really strange look and now he thinks I've got a crush on him, and I don't!"

Totally shameful?   Fair cause for a blush?   Oh, puh-lease! Get over it!

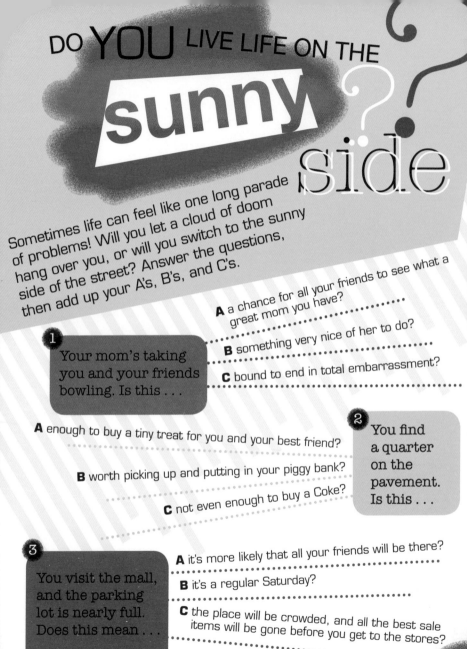

A Lots more cards will arrive tomorrow or be hand-delivered during the day.

B It's okay – birthdays aren't that important.

C Practically everyone forgot.

4

It's your birthday, and only two cards have arrived in the post. What's your take?

5

Your best friend is going to Disney World for her birthday. She's so excited. How do you feel?

A Pumped for your pal. You can't wait to hear all about it when she gets back.

B Pleased that she'll have a nice birthday.

C Really jealous that you're not going, but you cover it up by pretending you don't care.

A determined to do better next year and win?

B happy to be in the top three?

C convinced the winner must have had help to be that good?

6

You come in third in the school art competition. Are you . . .

Mostly A's

Wow! You certainly love to live in the sun. You have a great positive attitude – but don't worry if you feel sad sometimes; it's only natural!

Mostly B's

You certainly don't live your life in the clouds, but you're not basking in the sun either. You have an easygoing, balanced attitude that makes you great to be around.

Mostly C's

Hmmmm! You're a bit of a worrier. Try to think of the best possible outcome rather than the worst and see how much more fun you have!

all
star tmi

Starring ME!

Imagine you and your friends were papped. What would the captions say?

1) Take some photo-booth pictures of you and your friends.

2) Stick the photos in the boxes.

3) Fill the speech bubbles with what you COULD have been thinking or saying!

OMG
oh my gosh!

Interview your family.
What are their biggest-ever blushes?
Write them and rate them here!

"

"

Totally shameful?   Fair cause for a blush?   Oh, puh-lease! Get over it!

Totally shameful? **Fair cause for a blush?** **Oh, puh-lease! Get over it!**

Totally shameful? **Fair cause for a blush?** **Oh, puh-lease! Get over it!**

would you rather...

win one gold medal	or	win three bronze medals?
only have showers	or	**only have baths?**
be as big as a house	or	as small as a mouse?
laugh nonstop for an hour	or	**sneeze nonstop for an hour?**
sing your words for a day	or	say nothing for a day?
fly first class	or	**ride in a limousine?**
have no books	or	have no music?
grow an extra ear	or	**grow an extra nose?**

If you really, really

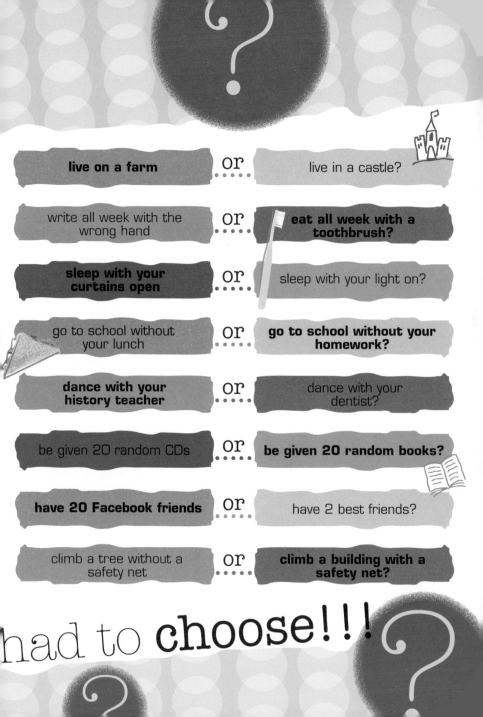

live on a farm	or	live in a castle?
write all week with the wrong hand	or	**eat all week with a toothbrush?**
sleep with your curtains open	or	sleep with your light on?
go to school without your lunch	or	**go to school without your homework?**
dance with your history teacher	or	dance with your dentist?
be given 20 random CDs	or	**be given 20 random books?**
have 20 Facebook friends	or	have 2 best friends?
climb a tree without a safety net	or	**climb a building with a safety net?**

had to **choose!!!**

How romantic are you?

start here

Pick a color.

pink →

Love songs - love 'em or leave 'em?

purple ↓

love →

Fluffy kittens - cute?

leave

totally

yes →

Ever sent a valentine?

not!

Do you believe in love at first sight?

yes

no →

no

Would you love to marry a prince or a rock star?

dreamy

prince

rock star

100% super-romantic! But watch that your heart doesn't get broken.

Walking hand in hand - eeeew! or dreamy?

eeeew!

flowers

You have a romantic side but you're no fool for love and not in a hurry to bag a boyf!

Best gift? Flowers or gift vouchers?

vouchers

bracelet

Charm bracelet or computer game?

game

You pick friends over dates every time. You might fall in love one day, but it looks like that won't be anytime soon!

love it
lose it!
nobody's 100% perfect

Time to put your favorite celebrities under the microscope! Write a list of your favorite stars, and then think of one thing you love about them and one thing that stops them from being totally perfect! For example, you might admire a star's great singing voice but would pass on her personal style!

name	love it	lose it!
	....	....

name	love it	lose it!
	....	....

name	love it	lose it!
	....	....

name	love it	lose it!
	....	....

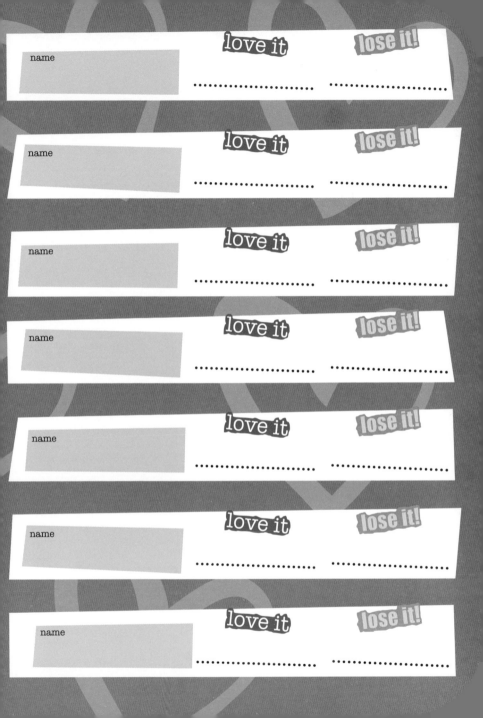

name   **love it**   **lose it!**

blush -o-meter

1

Your dad enters the room just as you are revealing your secret crush to your BFF. Do you . . .

say nothing to your dad and hope he didn't hear? **0**

brush it off as a joke you made up to see how he would react? **2**

refuse to look your dad in the face for at least a week? **4**

2

A friend has uploaded a clip of your school play on You Tube. Your friends look ultra glamorous, but the lighting has made your hair green, and you are singing totally off-key! Do you . . .

demand the clip is removed NOW? **3**

explain away the hair and singing as the result of a technical fault on your friend's phone? **2**

joke about how you'll volunteer to work backstage next year? **0**

3

You leave home in a hurry and grab your little sister's pink My Little Pony umbrella by mistake. You're with your coolest friends when it starts to rain. What do you do?

Open the umbrella and announce a new trend in retro-chic rainwear. **0**

Open the umbrella, but only after explaining to everyone that it absolutely does not belong to you and you only grabbed it by mistake. **2**

Pull your coat over your head – you'll keep dry(ish) and the pop-up ponies will stay in your bag! **3**

4

You've told your parents you just know you scored an A in your exam. Arghhh! You scored a D! It's time to confess – what do you tell them?

You feel kind of stupid but you'll definitely work harder next time. **1**

"I got a D," and then escape to your room really fast and put on your MP3 so you can't hear them knocking on your door. **3**

Try to persuade your parents that your teacher must have made a mistake (even though you know she probably didn't). **2**

Does your temperature rise when you're battling with a blush? Who's the coolest in a cringe-crisis? Take the test, add up your scores, and then check your blush-o-meter reading!

5

You and your best friend are exchanging gifts for the holidays. She's given you a beautiful necklace, a T-shirt, and a cute box, decorated with shells she collected from the beach. You're about to give her your gift — a bag of candy with a few missing because you were hungry on the way to her house. Ooops! What do you do?

Give her the candy and claim they are special because the missing ones were eaten by Zac Efron. **1**

Say you forgot her gift and promise to give it to her next week at school. **2**

Admit all you got her was some crummy candy and say you feel really bad about it. **3**

6

Your dad has joined an amateur theater group and is practicing his lines and singing really loudly, while you and your friends are trying to watch TV. Is this . . .

a good excuse to go to your friend's house instead? **2**

typical parent-like behavior – you just ignore him? **0**

the cause of a really big argument once your friends have gone home? **4**

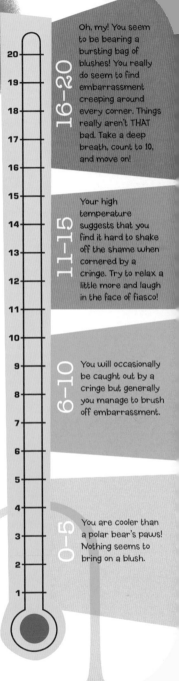

16–20
Oh, my! You seem to be bearing a bursting bag of blushes! You really do seem to find embarrassment creeping around every corner. Things really aren't THAT bad. Take a deep breath, count to 10, and move on!

11–15
Your high temperature suggests that you find it hard to shake off the shame when cornered by a cringe. Try to relax a little more and laugh in the face of fiasco!

6–10
You will occasionally be caught out by a cringe but generally you manage to brush off embarrassment.

0–5
You are cooler than a polar bear's paws! Nothing seems to bring on a blush.

OMG

Oh my gosh!

Interview your friends.
What are your buddies' biggest-ever blushes?
Write them and rate them here!

"

"

Totally shameful?   Fair cause for a blush? Oh, puh-lease! Get over it!

Totally shameful?   Fair cause for a blush?   Oh, puh-lease! Get over it!

Totally shameful?   Fair cause for a blush? Oh, puh-lease! Get over it!

fact or fancy?

Take turns answering the questions. The twist is that you **DON'T** have to tell the truth! Give your answers (the more details the better), and then have your friends guess whether you're dishing up Fact or Fancy!

Have you ever torn an item of clothing just so you didn't have to wear it?

Have you ever called your teacher "Mom" by mistake?

Have you ever sent a secret valentine?

Have you ever crushed on your sister's boyfriend?

What's the strangest thing in your pencil case?

What's the strangest thing in your room?

If you could live in any country in the world, which one would you pick?

What's the best grade you have ever achieved?

A++

Where's the most random place you've ever slept?

What's the worst item of clothing in your closet?

What's the most unusual pet you've ever owned?

Have you ever combined your name with your crush's to see what it would sound like if you were married?

What's the craziest thing you've ever done to skip school?

Have you ever eaten so much candy that you got sick?

Have you ever written a letter to a celebrity? What did you say?

If you could change your name, which name would you choose?

What's your favorite film of all time?

What would be your dream job?

Have you ever been caught gossiping about someone who's standing behind you?

Do you ever watch TV while your parents think you're sleeping?

What's the funniest trick you have ever played on your brother or sister?

shrug
or shriek!

How much embarrassment can you take?
Follow the flow - will you shriek or shrug?
If you shrug 'cuz you just don't care, go on to the
next space. If you shriek with embarrassment,
follow the blue arrow for your assessment!

You are at a restaurant for a
fancy meal with your family . . .

start here

Your mom has insisted you wear the totally unfashionable sweater your aunt bought for your birthday . . .

and the matching over-sized felt beret.

Okay, so your teacher has seen your fashion fiasco. But he's no style superhero, so who cares?

You are blushing way too early in this scenario! Okay, so you're not looking exactly fashion-forward, but who's going to see you?

You take your seats. Eeeek – your math teacher and his entire family are at the table next to yours. You were just totally too busy to do your math homework, and you told him your dog ate it!

Your overhear him replying, "Too bad it wasn't that nasty sweater and beret set!"

You have managed to keep calm to this point, which is admirable, but maybe you should just disappear under the table. Now!

Uh-oh! You've been busted! You certainly have cause to shriek! There's nothing worse than being cornered! But you've learned that honesty is definitely the best policy, so maybe it would have been cool to fess up and enjoy the rest of the evening.

Your teacher's son comes out of the restroom, and he's sooo cute! Uh-oh! Your teacher is telling him all about how you said your "dog" munched on your math!

You ditch the beret and take off your sweater, only to reveal the pink "I Love Zac Efron" nightshirt you put on 'cuz you were in a hurry!

He asks your mom if your dog is feeling okay. She tells him you don't have one!

You've kept your cool up to now but your shriek is 100% understandable and totally justified. Congrats for getting this far – time to fake an upset stomach and GO HOME!

would you rather...

live on a submarine	or	**live on a space station?**
eat with just a fork	or	eat with just a spoon?
wear a wig made out of spaghetti	or	**wear a wig made out of cotton candy?**
win an Olympic medal	or	win an Academy Award?
learn to ski	or	**learn to surf?**
build the world's biggest snowman	or	build the world's biggest sandcastle?
be given $1000 now	or	**be given $1 a week for the rest of your life?**
be a doctor	or	be a firefighter?

If you **really, really**

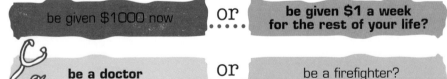

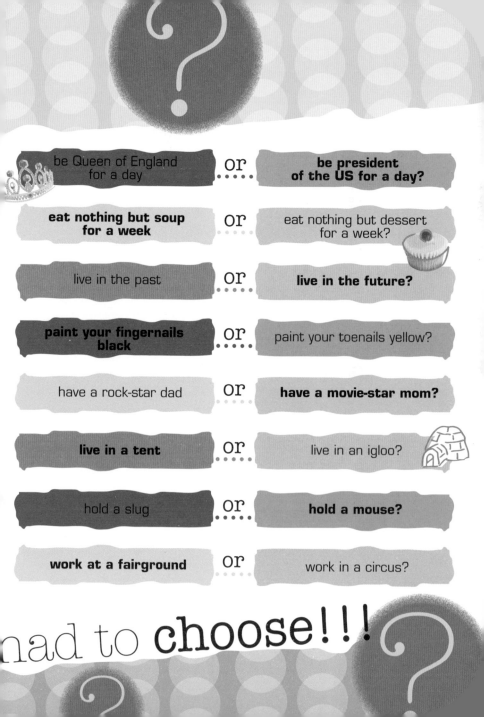

be Queen of England for a day **or** **be president of the US for a day?**

eat nothing but soup for a week **or** eat nothing but dessert for a week?

live in the past **or** **live in the future?**

paint your fingernails black **or** paint your toenails yellow?

have a rock-star dad **or** **have a movie-star mom?**

live in a tent **or** live in an igloo?

hold a slug **or** **hold a mouse?**

work at a fairground **or** work in a circus?

nad to **choose**!!!

wheel of shame!

Got a secret blush? Then it's time to fess up IN FRONT of your friends! First, answer one of the questions in the small circles; this will give you a number. Work your way clockwise around the wheel, starting at the yellow segment, until you land on your question. Do you dare to share, or is it totally TMI?

Take your age and add three.

Add together the digits of your house number. (So if it's 12, the answer is 1+2 = 3.)

Take the first letter of your name. What position is it in the alphabet? (If your name is Beth, the answer is two.)

Take the last number of your home phone or mobile number.

Subtract your age from your birth date. If you get to zero or below, take the yellow segment.

How many letters are there in your last name?

How many times can you clap your hands in five seconds? (Get someone to time you.)

fact or fancy?

Take turns answering the questions. The twist is that you DON'T have to tell the truth! Give your answers (the more details the better), and then have your friends guess whether you're dishing up Fact or Fancy!

Have you ever eaten a bug by mistake?

Who's the most famous person you have ever met?

Describe your secret talent.

Have you ever bought a present for someone and liked it so much that you kept if for yourself?

Have you ever eaten rotten food by mistake?

Have you ever licked food to stop anyone else from eating it?

Can you touch your nose with your tongue?

If you could have a celebrity sister, who would it be?

What's the nastiest thing you have ever smelled?

Would you ever have your nose pierced?

Are you double-jointed?

What's the craziest thing you've ever found in your hair?

Have you ever had a bird poop on you?

Have you ever made something up just to impress your crush?

What's the worst thing you have ever drunk by mistake?

Have you ever begged your mom to change her outfit? What was she wearing?

Have you ever walked into a boy's locker room by mistake?

Have you ever been in an elevator when someone's passed gas?

If you had a million dollars, what's the first thing you would buy?

What's the most embarrassing thing that's ever happened to you in front of your friends?

What's the most random thing you've ever sat on?

good day bad day

The following situations could have any outcome. Think of the best that could happen (good day) and the worst (bad day).

Happy ending or totally TMI!!

good day

bad day

It's a Saturday afternoon and you're home and totally bored. Your phone rings. Who is it?

good day

bad day

You've won a prize in a magazine competition. What is it?

good day

bad day

Your dad's taking you to the cinema for a treat. What are you going to see?

good day

bad day

You've always wanted a pet, and your mom has finally agreed! What's it going to be?

bad day

Your parents have decorated your room as a surprise. What's the theme?

good day   bad day

You get no text messages all day, then you get two at once! Who are they from?

good day   bad day

There's one piece of chocolate left in the box. What flavor is it?

good day   bad day

You've been given a role in the school play! Who are you going to play?

good day   bad day

Your mom bought you a new dress. What style is it?

good day   bad day

The elevator in the mall has broken down! Who's in the elevator with you?

good day   bad day

mall

school ?

or friend's house

Check out the situation, and then decide the **best** place and the **worst** place it could happen from the three choices.

| **Losing a tooth** | Mall | School | Friend's house |

| **Having bad breath** | Elevator | Theme park | School |

| **Having a headache** | Park | School | Movie theater |

| **Cutting your finger** | Swimming pool | School | Theme park |

| **Wearing your least favorite clothes** | Mall | Movie theater | Restaurant |

| **Laughing so much you pee in your pants** | Restaurant | Swimming pool | Theme park |

Argument with your brother or sister	Mall	Theater	Park
Locking yourself in the bathroom	Friend's house	School	Mall
Losing your voice	Movie theater	Theme park	Dentist's
Having an upset stomach	Restaurant	School	Theme park
Text message from your crush	Theater	Restaurant	Elevator
Ripping your pants	Restaurant	Park	Mall
Spilling Coke on yourself	Theme park	Restaurant	Mall
Getting toilet paper stuck to your shoe	Mall	Restaurant	Friend's house
Getting food stuck in your hair	Restaurant	Mall	School
Being caught in the rain	Sports field	Beach	Theme park
Having a booger hanging from your nose	Dentist's	Elevator	Restaurant

shrug
or shriek!

How much embarrassment can you take?
Follow the flow – will you shriek or shrug?
If you shrug 'cuz you just don't care, go on to the
next space. If you shriek with embarrassment,
follow the purple arrow for your assessment!

Your fave band is playing at the mall, and
your mom has agreed to take you to see
them. Fantastic!

start here

Your little brother
has insisted on
coming too, and
he doesn't even
like them!

He's bringing
his best friend
Ryan – he's
really annoying!

This situation is perhaps
more irritating than
embarrassing. It might
not be ideal but you should
try not to let this set-back
spoil your day!

Having to cope with your
mom's singing is bad
enough, but telling you she's
crushing on your favorite
boy babe is just plain
disturbing! But at least your
friends aren't in the car to
hear your mom's singing or
her revolting revelations,
so maybe you should have
held out longer. Things can
always be worse . . .

Your mom has brought along
a CD of the band to play in
the car and she's singing
along. Now she's telling you
she's totally crushed on the
lead singer! Eeew! TMI, Mom!

Uh-oh! Seeing he has an audience, Ryan puts his arm around you, gives you a big kiss, and tells your buddies you're dating! That is *so* not true! Just as you manage to shake off Ryan, the band starts to play and your mom starts dancing in a weird, retro way.

This situation is not good, so maybe it was best to bail. You could hide in the restroom, but you'll miss the show, which is a shame . . .

This is very embarrassing but not the end of the world. Look, apart from your mom's singing and crush confession nobody's actually done anything to embarrass you, so maybe you should have held on a little longer.

Now your mom is telling everyone how excited she is to be seeing your fave band!

No, no, no, no, no! Your mom is onstage doing a totally embarrassing smoochy dance with the lead singer. Who let her up there?

You arrive at the mall and get a place at the front near the stage. Your buddies have arrived and are taking their seats next to you. They start to snicker when they see you are with rotten Ryan!

So it turns out Ryan's dad runs the mall and set the situation up as a surprise for your mom! Now you and Ryan have been called to join the band onstage! Before you know it you are rocking out with your mom and Ryan, and everyone can see!

This is quite possibly the worst situation you will ever find yourself in! If you are not shrieking at this mortifying madness, you are totally un-blushable!

DO YOU give 110%?

Will you give everything to achieve your goals?

1 You have half an hour before your favorite TV show and at least an hour's math homework left to finish for tomorrow. What do you do?

A Ditch the homework and watch TV. You can finish your fractions later.

B Record the show and finish your homework.

C Ask your mom and do what she says.

2 You are auditioning for a part in your school play and have just three days left to learn your lines. Do you . . .

A try to find time, but end up staying up late the night before your audition?

B set aside some time each night to memorize your lines?

C practice every night – if your friends offer to help you?

3 When you got your first phone, did you . . .

A only learn to text when people started sending you messages?

B learn to text right away?

C wait for someone to offer to teach you how to text?

4

Which of these skills would you love to learn the most?

A Multitasking (doing lots of things at once)

B Speed-reading (reading a book in super quick time)

The art of persuasion – so you can get people to do things for you!

5

You've won third place in the school swim-a-thon. Do you . . .

A feel good about your achievement and wonder if you could have come first if you'd trained a little harder?

B keep on practicing and go for first place next year?

C enter again next year, as long as your friends do?

6

Which of these is MOST important in a true best friend?

A Sense of adventure

B Honesty

C They're always there if you need them.

fun!

Mostly A's

You work hard but can be distracted if something more interesting comes along. You sometimes need a gentle nudge to move you to action, but more often than not you'll be happy with your achievements.

Mostly B's

If you're not giving it 110% you're giving it something very close. Your fantastic focus means you're set to achieve your goals!

Mostly C's

It's not that you can't do something – more often than not you just don't want to or don't see the point until someone shows you. It's a super casual outlook that can minimize stress, but it won't give you a great sense of achievement!

cringe man

Just like regular hangman, you need two players.
Take one of the sentences below and think of a word to fill the
gap. Next, put a dash for each letter under one of the "cringe
men." Your opponent has to guess the word by gradually
revealing the letters. Each time they guess a letter correctly fill
in a dash, and when they get it wrong draw over one of the faint
cringeman lines. If they guess the word before the cringeman
is complete, they win – if they don't, you win!

My sleepover was totally ruined when my brother crashed
the party wearing a _____!

I looked under the sofa and came face to face with the biggest _____
I have ever seen!

I felt so stupid when I realised I'd left my phone in the _____.

The pizza tasted great apart from the _____ on the top!

Eeeew! I found an old _____ at the bottom of my bag!

Cringe! The wind blew my new hairstyle and I looked just like a _____!

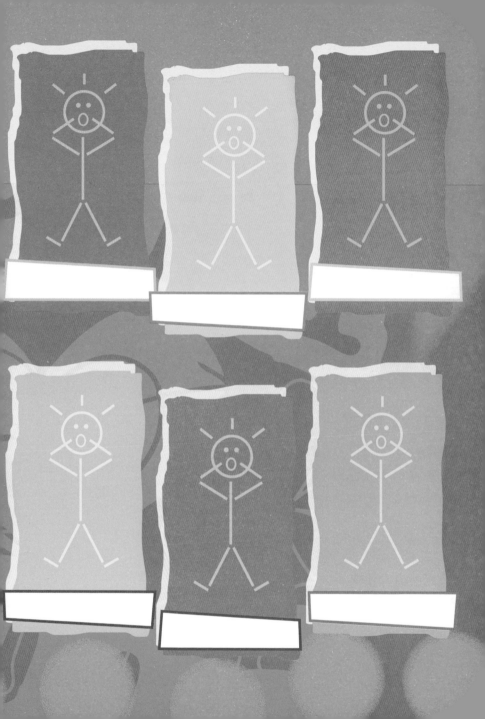

all star tmi

Famous people just love to **DISH!**

1) Flip through your favorite magazine.

2) Find a pic of your favorite (or least favorite!) celeb. Cut it out and paste it in the box.

3) Fill the speech bubbles with what YOU think they're saying!

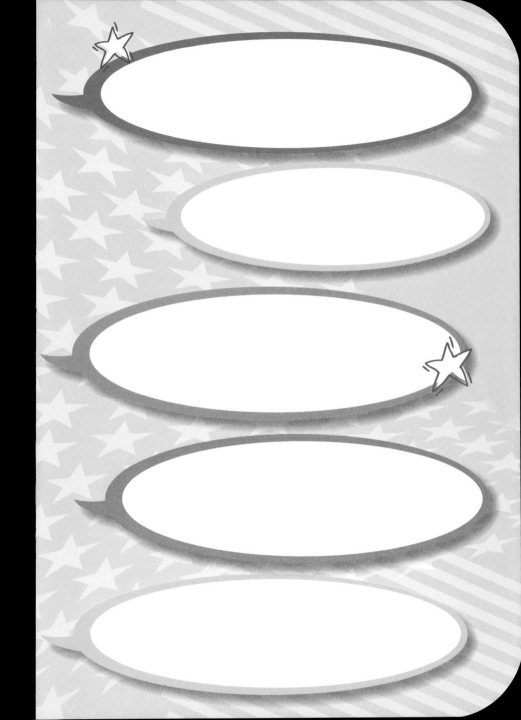

OMG

Oh my gosh!

Bag a blush or brush it off? Read these stories, and you be the judge!

SHOPPING CART CATASTROPHE!

"I was at the grocery store with my mom. She gave me a long list of groceries to get while she chatted with her friend. I was listening to my MP3, so I wasn't really concentrating on what I was doing. I had just finished loading up the cart with toilet paper when I looked up and realized that it wasn't my cart – it belonged to a total stranger! And he was cute! I nearly died."

Totally shameful?　　Fair cause for a blush?　　Oh, puh-lease! Get over it!

SHOW SHOCKER!

"I love performing in end-of-the-year shows and was proud to have the lead role in our production of *Hairspray!* On opening night, I walked out onto the stage for the opening number, opened my mouth, and completely forgot the words to the song! I should have just hummed along, but instead I tried to make up my own words. I ended up singing something about how much I loved my kitten and what I was having for dinner. It was soooo embarrassing, especially when I said I was having fish sticks and someone shouted back, "No, you're not, you're having hot dogs!" Oh, the SHAME!

Totally shameful?　　Fair cause for a blush?　　Oh, puh-lease! Get over it!

DANCING DISASTER!

"I was in a hurry to get to the park to meet my friends. Most of my good clothes were in the wash so I pulled on an old, baggy pair of sweatpants. A little later, some boys were trying to impress us with their street dancing. I decided to join in and stood on a bench pretending it was a stage. I was throwing some totally funky shapes and thinking how hot I looked when I slipped on some spilled water. I tried to regain my balance but instead went bottom-first into the bin next to the bench, snagging my sweats on a bit of old wire! As I pulled myself up, the wire pulled my sweats down, exposing my flowery pink underwear! Totally shameful!"

Totally shameful?   Fair cause for a blush?   Oh, puh-lease! Get over it!

DISGUSTING DISH!

"It was my best friend's birthday, so I decided to bake her a cake. My mom bought me a cake mix, so it was really easy. I didn't have time to frost the cake, so I decided to sprinkle sugar on the top instead. It looked totally tasty and I felt really proud as I cut my BFF a big slice. She took one bite, made a really ugly face, and immediately spat it out! OMG – I had put salt on top of the cake instead of sugar!"

Totally shameful?   Fair cause for a blush?   Oh, puh-lease! Get over it!

fact or fancy?

Take turns answering the questions. The twist is that you **DON'T** have to tell the truth! Give your answers (the more details the better), and then have your friends guess whether you're dishing up Fact or Fancy!

What's the most unusual thing you have ever kissed?

If you could have a secret superpower what would it be?

What's the craziest competition you have ever entered?

Do you keep a secret diary?

Have you ever given your mom a makeover?

What's the grossest thing you have ever done when you thought nobody was looking?

Have you ever been carsick?

What's the funniest thing you've ever seen on the Internet?

Describe your dad's worst shoes.

What's the lowest grade you have ever received?

Who was your first crush?

Have you ever colored your own hair?

If you could be invisible for a day, where would you go?

What's the most extreme thing you've ever done to skip gym?

What's the worst thing you've ever found in your your coat pocket?

Have you ever secretly tried your mom's makeup?

Have you ever been caught dancing in front of a mirror?

Have you ever talked to your toys?

If you could have a celebrity brother who would it be?

What's the most random gift you've ever received?

What's the craziest fib you've ever told?

If you could marry any celebrity, who would it be?

would you rather...

kiss a boy	...or...	**kiss a frog?**
join the police	or	join the coast guard?
have cornflakes in your socks	...or...	**have cornflakes in your hair?**
go to school on roller skates	...or...	go to school on a pogo stick?
be stung by a wasp	or	**be bitten by a snake?**
dance with Beyoncé	or...	dance with Pink?
eat chicken for breakfast	...or...	**eat cornflakes for dinner?**
wear false nails to school	or	wear false lashes to school?

If you really, really

put your hands in a bucket of snails **or** **hold your hands in the air for an hour?**

live underground **or** live underwater?

eat no chocolate for a year **or** **watch no TV for a year?**

fly like a bird **or** swim like a dolphin?

eat bread without butter **or** **eat fries without ketchup?**

be a bus driver **or** be an ambulance driver?

have six brothers **or** **have six sisters?**

go to bed early **or** get up early?

had to **choose!!!**

OMG

oh my gosh!

Confess your biggest blushes here –
then ask your BFF to rate them!

"

"

Totally shameful?   Fair cause for a blush?   Oh, puh-lease! Get over

Totally shameful? **Fair cause for a blush?** Oh, puh-lease! Get over it!

Totally shameful? **Fair cause for a blush?** Oh, puh-lease! Get over it!

totally tmi

Check your watches! You have 30 seconds to spill nonstop on any of the subjects below – without dishing up **Too Much Information!** All you need are your friends and a dice.

Cut out the TMI cards. You have six, but you can make more if you need them or don't want to cut up the book.

Roll the dice to find out which question you must answer first!

You must talk for 30 seconds on the subject without stopping to think. If you stop, you're out! Don't hold back – your friends can hold up their TMI card at any point if what you say is just too weird, too crazy, or just plain gross! And if they do, you're out!

1 What's your worst habit?

2 What is the worst meal ever?

3 Talk about the celeb you'd most like to date!

4 What's the most embarrassing thing you have ever seen your parents do?

5 Describe the smelliest place you have ever been.

6 What's the worst thing you could possibly wear to a wedding?